Jacqueline Mines

IN SCHOOL SUSPENSION ENRICHMENT CURRICULUM

ENRICHING LIVES OF CHILDREN ONE CHILD AT A TIME

Breezeway Books

© 2018, 2013 Jacqueline Mines

All rights reserved. No part of this publication may be reproduced or transmitted in any form or by any means electronic or mechanical, including photocopy, recording, or any information storage and retrieval system, without permission in writing from the copyright owner.

Requests for permission to make copies of any part of this work should be mailed to Permissions Department, Breezeway Books, 7970 NW 4th Place, Plantation, FL 33324

ISBN: 978-1-62550-575-0

Library of Congress Control Number: 2013919150

MOTTO FOR STUDENT SUCCESS

By Jacqueline Mines

I am special and uniquely created. I know now, more so than ever before, that
I must work hard from this day forward to achieve my own destiny.
I am clearer now than ever before that I, yes I,
have the power to become anything I want.
I am the driving force for accomplishing my own goals,
And no one but me can determine my future path.
I choose to do what is right; I choose to live by the rules.
I fully understand that the choices I make today
Will help to shape the decisions I make tomorrow.
I acknowledge and accept that being a failure is never an option.
This promise I make to myself.
I pledge to myself that my future will be bright.
I understand that it's going to take
Hard work, perseverance, and purpose,
But I also know:
I can and I know I will
Be the best that I can be.
Therefore, I strongly believe that I will be
Victorious in all of my efforts!
I will never settle for being a victim because my future is too brilliant.
I am going after it vigorously. There is nothing I can't do, but there is a lot I can do.
I am ready to put aside everything and everyone who tries to block my success.
I am aware that it starts and ends with me!
I understand education is the path that leads to my success.
It is the only road I must travel.
I know there will be obstacles, but I will not lose focus.
As I approach the end of this road, I will start to see different signs:
Five miles left; four miles; three miles; two miles; now one mile left…
Finally, I see:
"Final Destination"
You have reached your "Path to Success"

A job well done!

"A personal pledge, just for me"

Today, I will do my best in group session.
I will listen to others when they are speaking.
I will follow directions.
I will be honest with myself.
I will respect the rights of others.
I will be open to learning.
I will be open to making the changes I need to be a better person.
I know it's up to me to do what's right.
I will take personal ownership of my actions.
I will do what I need to do to correct behaviors that obstruct my growth.
I will not be judgmental toward others.
I will respect the opinions of others.

Ground Rules for Group Session

These rules will be decided by the group. Once they are determined, everyone will be expected to follow each rule. Remember, you set these rules.

Two sample ground rules:

1. <u>No talking without being recognized by the facilitator</u>
2. <u>Turn off all cell phones</u>
3. _____
4. _____
5. _____
6. _____
7. _____
8. _____
9. _____
10. _____

Expected Student Behaviors

✸ I believe everyone deserves a safe, supportive, and orderly learning environment.

✸ I am encouraged and appreciate the opportunity to be taught and the opportunities for new learning to occur.

✸ I will do my part by creating opportunities to practice and succeed by being responsible and making effective choices in order to reach my academic potential.

I will show respect for...

Myself by:

- Attending school regularly and being on time.
- Following my teachers, administrators, and other adults' rules and directions
- Doing my schoolwork and homework neatly and completely
- Working on positive behaviors and making better choices
- Remaining at school doing school hours, unless I have permission to leave school
- Learning from the consequences of my behavior and behaviors of others
- Choosing never to use tobacco, alcohol, drugs, or weapons or bring them to school
- Dressing in a way that is appropriate for the learning environment

I will show respect for…

Others by:

- Being understanding of other's feelings
- Using positive words with others (no putdowns)
- Treating others as I would like to be treated (respectful)
- Not bullying or threatening others, and reporting it when I see it happening
- Being honest, by telling the truth, and by admitting to things I have done

- **Working with others in a positive manner**
- **Keeping my hands to myself**
- **Refraining from using profanity**
- **Managing negative behaviors, feelings, and emotions**
- **Using a respectful, positive, and considerate tone of voice and body language when speaking to others**
- **Paying close attention and listening carefully when others are speaking to me**

List of Feeling Words and Expressions of Self-Reflection

From this list on the next page, pick the word that best describe how you feel. **If you do not see a word that describes how you are feeling, pick your own word.**

GLAD	SAD	MAD	AFRAID	OTHER
content	bugged	uncomfortable	shy	inquisitive
glad	blah	annoyed	startled	curious
pleased	blue	irritated	uneasy	sassy
playful	gloomy	mean	tense	weird
cheerful	rotten	crabby	anxious	confused
giddy	sad	cranky	worried	moody
calm	unhappy	grumpy	concerned	small
comfortable	empty	grouchy	timid	quiet
cozy	jealous	safe	embarrassed	relaxed
confident	responsible	strong	concerned	peaceful
caring	bored	delighted	disappointed	disgusted
peaceful	alarmed	hurt	ticked	scarred
jolly	lost	mad	afraid	tickled
bubbly	sorry	angry	frightened	silly
happy	ashamed	smoldering	fearful	frisky
loved	down	blissful	miserable	helpless
joyful	lonely	hot	threatened	discouraged
proud	frustrated	shaky	impatient	awful
hopeless	shaken	disturbed	depressed	ecstatic
thankful	petrified	withdrawn	depressed	wonderful
delightful	heartbroken	panicky	explosive	terrific
charming	horrified	horrified	unloved	alive
amusing	jubilant	violent	enraged	grateful
enchanting	terrified	sparkly	doomed	satisfied
delicious	fuming	furious	self-conscious	misplaced
enjoyable	attitude	emotional	uncertain	unforgiving

LIFE SKILLS BUILDING BLOCKS
Designed to Last for a Lifetime

STUDENT ACHIEVEMENT AND SUCCESS
Lagging skills will destroy our children's future

1. COMMUNICATION — Page 1

2. DECISION MAKING — Page 8

3. SELF-ESTEEM — Page 20

4. VALUES — Page 28

5. HOW TO HANDLE CONFLICT — Page 33

6. PEER PRESSURE — Page 43

7. GANG AFFILIATION — Page 50

8. BULLYING — Page 59

Children who are suspended are often from a population that is the least likely to be supervised while on suspension. It's time to keep our children in school.

When I make positive behavior choices, I can be successful.
However, if I do not make positive behavior choices,
I agree to receive intervention services to help me learn to make better choices.

TOPIC OVERVIEWS

1. COMMUNICATION

Students will learn that proper communication is the most critical skill for advancing. They will learn the effectiveness of proper communication skills and improve their ability to communicate with their families, teachers, peers, and others. Students will understand and learn how proper body language and good listening skills will provide better outcomes and minimize bad situations. Students will learn that active listening is essential to understanding. The objective is to make sure students learn that communicating demands both hearing and being heard.

"The presence of an effective communication pattern is one of the most frequently mentioned characteristics of strong families."
—*Swihart, 1988*

2. DECISION MAKING

"I make choices today, and the choices make me tomorrow." Facing difficulties and having to make difficult choices are a part of life, like breathing. Where I am today is the result of the choices I made yesterday, and where I am tomorrow is the result of the choices I make today. You may be confronted with challenging or threatening situations, but it is your **responsibility** to make the right choices. The objective will be for students to understand and learn the do's and don'ts of making better choices by learning to stop, think, and then speak.

"It is not only for what we do that we are held responsible, but also for what we do not do."
—*Chinese proverb*

3. SELF-ESTEEM

High self-esteem – feeling good about oneself – makes it easier to meet life's challenges. Students who believe in their ability to succeed are most often able to do so. Good self-esteem provides a basis for feeling stronger. Students will learn how to encourage and foster high self-esteem, learn to accept some failure as normal, and remain resilient in their efforts to keep trying. The objective will be for students to learn how to cope with day-to-day challenges and problems. The training objective will also be for students to be able to look toward their futures with excitement and confidence while working on fulfilling their goals. Students will learn that with high self-esteem, they are not likely to let others make their decisions for them or influence them to do things they do not want to do.

"Experience is not what happens to a person. It is what a person does with what happens to him."
—*Aldous Huxley*

4. VALUES

Values are a reflection of your culture and your unique heritage. Being clear about your values empowers you to establish priorities and make decisions. What you learn in your childhood serves you throughout life. Families should guide your growth and education, while offering love and protection. When your family and your home are strong, you can be more hopeful about the future. The objective will be for students to learn how values influence choices. They will learn how values help to shape what they perceive and how it influence their goals.

"If you wish to know the mind of a man, listen to his words."
—*Chinese proverb*

5. HANDLING CONFLICT

Students will learn that conflict is a normal part of human interaction when people have different values. They will learn that negative conflict should be avoided. Students will be provided with positive skills for handling conflict. The objective will be for students to learn how to increase and improve their motivational skills to do well which will help them deal with pressure in a more proactive manner.

"Coming together is a beginning, staying together is progress, working together is success."
—*Henry Ford*

6. PEER PRESSURE

Making good decisions can be difficult in the school environment, especially when others get involved. Fellow students (classmates or friends) are called "peers"; when they try to influence you, it is called **"peer pressure."** Even adults deal with peer pressure. The objective will be for students to learn that being influenced to do good things can be good, but being influenced to do something bad is not good.

When the character of a man is not clear to you, look at his friends.
—*Molière*

7. GANG AFFILIATION

Students will explore how they think their parents feel when they discover their child is associating with a gang. They will learn the seriousness of their commitment and the seriousness of trying to separate once they join a gang. The objective will be to provide students with more rewarding alternatives and activities. Students will learn how involvement in a gang affects them, their families, teachers, peers, and many others.

"Nonviolence is a powerful and just weapon…which cuts without wounding and ennobles the man who wields it. It is a sword that heals."
—*Martin Luther King, Jr.*

8. BULLYING HURTS

Bullying among school-aged youth is increasingly recognized as an important problem affecting the well-being and social functioning of students in school, out of school, and on school buses. While a certain amount of conflict and harassment is typical of youth peer relations, bullying presents a more serious threat to healthy development. The objective will be for students to learn the cons of bullying and the impact it can have on the lives of others.

> *"Young bullies carry a one-in-four chance of having a criminal record by age 30."*
> —Leonard Enron and Rowell Huesmans

THIS SUCKS! IT'S JUST A WASTE OF MY TIME.

I'LL JUST SIT HERE.

I REALLY DON'T CARE IF I AM SUSPENDED.

WHATEVEEEER!

 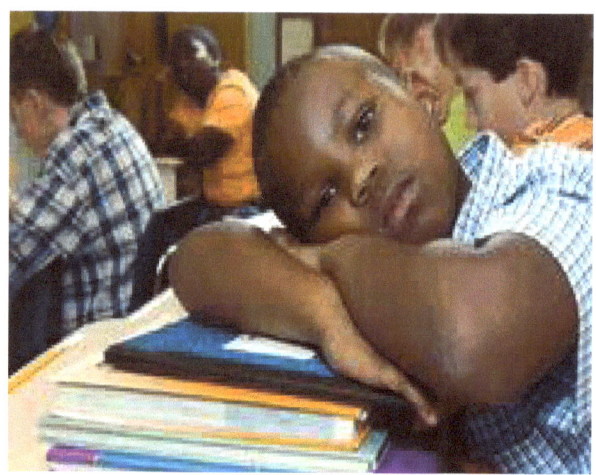

Suspension could be better, if...
I got to go home. Hey, I could play my video games, visit my friends on the street corner, sleep late, have friends over, go watch a gang jump in new gang members.

Instead, I have to sit in a room watching the "warden" read her or his book or the newspaper. I wouldn't mind being suspended if I didn't have to sit in this stupid room. There's a lot I could be doing instead of sitting here doing nothing. **No one cares, anyway. Why should** I?

Communication Skills

LESSON 1

By the end of this lesson, I will:

1) Understand the importance of communication
2) Understand the concept of "communication"
3) Understand the positive and negative effects of body language
4) Understand the power of listening
5) Explore new ways to communicate effectively

1. Effective Communication

Communication means, "To impart, to pass along, to make known, to give and receive information." The word *communication* comes from the Latin word *communist*, which means, "**Common.**" Therefore, when we attempt to communicate, we are trying to establish **commonality** with another individual or group. Communication is much more than just the exchange of words.

Now we will review and discuss each of the phases of communication listed below:

- What we say
- How we say it
- Why we say it
- The way we say it
- What we neglect to say
- Our body expressions
- Our facial expressions
- Our eye movements
- Our nonverbal expressions
- Our tone-of-voice
- Our listening habits
- Our hand movement

As students, you see the world as a place of infinite possibilities, full of new people and new situations. This is why it is so important to understand that your ability to understand and be understood depends on how well you are able to communicate with each other.

We will discuss every aspect of being a good communicator. We will also have open dialogs, do role-playing, and critique each other by observing each other's listening skills, body language, vocal tones, eye contact, facial expressions, etc.

"Nine-tenths of the serious controversies that arise in life result from misunderstanding, from one man not knowing the facts which to the other man seem important, or other-wise failing to appreciate his point of view."

—*Justice Louis D. Brandeis*

A major part of effective communication:

2. Body Language

It is critical that attention is given to your **body language** and **tone of voice** when communicating.

Let's now do some role-playing by communicating only with your body expression. Afterward, as a group, we will discuss what each person said, based only on nonverbal expression.

As mentioned before, communication includes both verbal and **nonverbal language**. Words are the tools of verbal language. However, nonverbal language has many components. **Posture,** the **position of our bodies, and facial expression** all come into play. Other elements include **tone of voice, gestures, mannerisms, and behavior and actions**.

Look at this picture. Based on what you see, what do you think the class's body language is expressing to their teacher?

Monitoring your body language is very important. Body language can be used to your advantage or disadvantage. Below are a few questions. We will review each and have dialog regarding the importance of each one.

- How do you use your body language to convey a message?
- What do you do when you're angry?
- How do you express yourself when you are sad?
- What are your actions when you are happy?
- How could you use body language to your advantage?

If you want to be taken seriously, take yourself seriously. Self-improvement is the basis for individual development. Pay close attention to your body language to send the right message to others. On the next page, we will discuss the importance of active listening, and the way it will improve your communication skills.

3. Active Listening

Active listening is essential to effective communication and vital to hearing and being heard. In active listening, judgment is suspended, and the listener uses empathy to try to understand the other person's experiences, feelings, and point of view.

I am listening to my dad and receiving advice that will benefit me throughout my life. I am actively listening, looking him in his eyes, and showing him I am interested in what he is saying. Active listening really does work! I encourage you to try it, too.

Of the four language arts, listening skills are used more than the other three skills combined.

The ability to listen well is essential for success and acquiring information to process and communicate to others. To be good listeners, remember the following six steps.

Let's review each step. Afterwards, we will discuss each.

- **CLARIFY** - Ask questions to confirm what the other person said.
- **RESTATE** - Repeat in your own words what the person said.
- **REFLECT** - In your own words, tell the person what you think he or she is experiencing.
- **SUMMARIZE** - Reiterate the major ideas, themes, and feelings the person has expressed.
- **VALIDATE** - Show appreciation for the person's efforts and acknowledge the value of talking.

Look! Two ears and one mouth.

**Remember, we were created with two ears and one mouth—
YOU CAN FILL IN THE REST.**

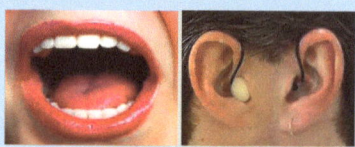

In other word, we should be listening more than talking!

4. Below are key strategies for building and strengthening your communication skills:
   - **Avoid letting aggravations accumulate.**
   - **Be honest, but not accusatory.**
   - **When you argue, do so constructively.**
   - **Put yourself in the other person's shoes.**
   - **Accept feelings; do not judge them.**

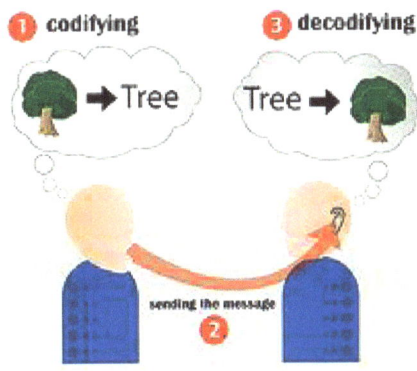

You speak, and the other person listens.

They speak, and you listen.

Talking over each other is never an option!

Summary

Now that you've had an opportunity to discuss the importance of every phase of effective communication skills, you now need to practice.

Improving your communication skills will open opportunities for you in your personal life and benefit you in and out of school. Others will respect you more, look up to you, find you to be a person with character and a bright future.

5. Self-Evaluation Checklist–

Everyone is required to participate in this exercise. The main objective is so that others can learn from your learning and become better communicators themselves.

Do the following statements apply to you? Mark each statement "T" for True or "F" for False. Be honest. This is the only way you are going to learn.

1. ____I clearly say what I mean.

2. ____I am an attentive and sympathetic listener.

3. ____When I do not understand something, I ask questions.

4. ____I let other people finish talking before I speak.

5. ____I am straightforward and forthright in expressing my thoughts and feelings.

6. ____I rarely use sarcasm or insults.

7. ____I willingly listen to the ideas and feelings of others.

8. ____When stating an opinion, I use words like "I think" and "It seems to me."

9. ____I seldom get angry or hostile when someone disagrees with me.

10. ____I am sensitive to nonverbal signals like tone of voice and body language.

**The more "TRUES" you have, the more skillful a communicator you are.
But the fewer trues you have, the more work you have to do.**

How do you think you can help others learn to be better communicators?

Let's have a group discussion on what you've learned from this exercise.

The Four Communication Skills

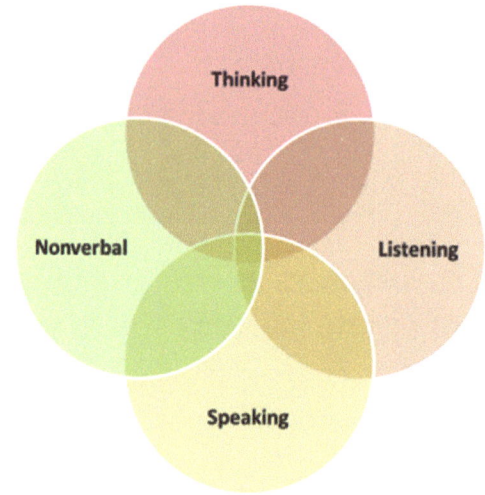

Review these two questions, and afterwards, we will discuss your answer.

Are there aspects of communication that you need to work on? Yes ___ No ___

If so, please list five areas in which you need to improve.

1. _____

2. _____

3. _____

4. _____

5. _____

2. **Explain the difference between listening and hearing.**

_____
_____
_____
_____
_____
_____

Use this space to record what you learned from our discussion:

Additional comments/Reflection:

_____
_____
_____
_____
_____
_____

Congratulations! You have just completed training to become a better communicator.

You should be proud.

Decision Making

LESSON 2

By the end of this lesson, I will:

1) Understand that I have the power of choice
2) Understand the consequences of bad choices and their effects.
3) Learn to rise above my emotions.
4) Understand when others are influencing me in a negative way.

The choice is yours.

"I make choices today, and those choices make me tomorrow."

Facing problems and making difficult choices are a part of life.

Where you are today is the result of the choices you made yesterday, and where you are tomorrow is the result of the choices you make today.

When you are confronted with challenging or threatening situations, it is your responsibility to make the right choices. Within the freedom to choose are gifts that make you uniquely human. These gifts separate you from other living creations.

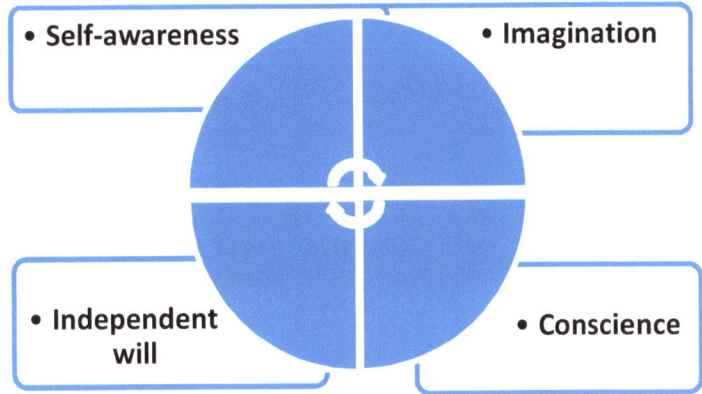

Let's review and discuss each gift.

Self-awareness:

Think about your mood. Can you identify it?

- ❖ What are you feeling? Explain as clearly as you can.
- ❖ How would you describe your present mental state?
- ❖ Now think for a minute about your mind.
- ❖ Is it quick and alert?

Your ability to do what you just did is uniquely human. Other creatures do not possess this ability. It is called **self-awareness,** or the ability to think about and control your thought process.

This is why you can make or break habits.

Did you know you had the power to do this? Yes ___ No___

What would be your choice? Would you do good or bad? It's up to you. You have the power to choose!

Place a check mark next to your choice. As of this day, I choose to do:
Good____ Bad____

Because? Please explain your decision:
_____
_____
_____
_____
_____

You can choose to **learn**____ or **fail**____. You can choose to be **successful** ____or **unsuccessful** ____. The choice is yours. Check your preferences and be prepared to discuss.

Keep in mind the following: **You are not your various moods. You are not even your thoughts.** The fact that you can think before reacting separates you from animals.

In addition to **self-awareness,** you have an imagination. What does imagination means to you?

> You have the ability to create in your mind beyond your present reality. To be able to envision the outcome of an event even before it takes place.

Everyone has an imagination. Some people use their imaginations to plan for their futures; some use their imaginations to do evil; some use their imaginations to see themselves doing good or bad. How do you use your imagination?

Please explain you answer:

_____
_____
_____
_____

Now we will discuss how your conscience works and how it affects your actions.

> Your conscience is the deep inner awareness of the right or wrong principles that govern your behavior.

Your conscience can reward you for good behavior and convict you for doing wrong.

Have you ever felt the difference? Yes__ No __ Not sure__

Please explain your answer.

_____
_____
_____
_____

Now we will discuss your independent free will: It offers you the ability to do or not do, to fight or walk away from a fight, to learn or not learn, to study or fail, to attend school or stay home, to live with conflict or to be free of conflict. Use your free will to choose what is right or correct. You may do as you please, but keep in mind that free will comes with consequences, which can be good or bad.

In Summary:
Be aware of **your self-awareness**, and remember you can **imagine** the outcome of your actions. You can consciously decide whether your decisions are right or wrong. You also can exercise your **free and independent will** to react or not react to situations.

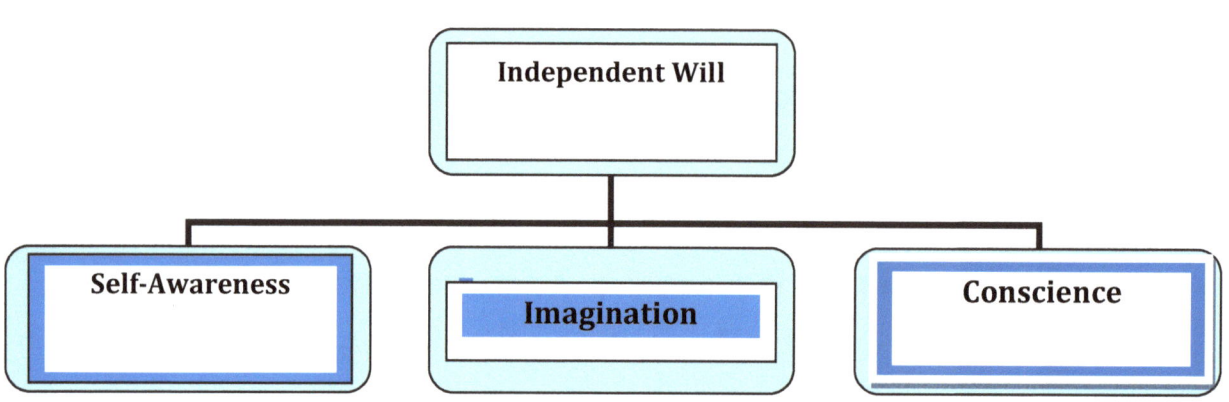

LET'S RECAP

1. <u>**Self-awareness**</u>: having perception and knowledge of one's self; having the ability to analyze one's own thinking and actions

2. <u>**Imagination**</u>: the act or power of forming a mental image of something not visible to the senses or not previously known or experienced

3. <u>**Conscience**</u>: the moral right and wrong of one's acts or motives

4. <u>**Independent Will**</u>: offers you free will; the ability to do or not to do

Now let's read a story about a young man whose life changed almost overnight because of a decision **he made**. He fell victim to some of the **influences** that surrounded him, and he is now suffering the **consequences** of his choices.

THIS LETTER SHOULD BE READ ALOUD TO THE GROUP!

Sixteen years ago, I made the biggest mistake of my life. I became a drug dealer. I knew it was wrong, but I did it anyway. I now realize that my reasons for selling drugs were no reasons at all. I never considered the individuals I hurt or the things I did out of greed. I was more concerned about my reputation, driving flashy cars to get noticed, sporting a Rolex to be called "the Man," buying expensive clothes to build my low self-esteem, and carrying guns because that's the only time I had courage.

Ask me if it was worth it, and I'll tell you, "Hell, No!" It was suicidal, a real-life nightmare, minus sleep. Ask me why I sold drugs, and I will tell you the truth – peer pressure, ignorance, stupidity, insanity, and a lack of love for myself and humanity. Which brings me to you if you choose a life of crime, ask if it is worth throwing your precious life away – your only life. It takes one bad decision for your life to go in a negative direction that can lead to suffering and long-term consequences.

Gangbanging is becoming more popular. If that's the avenue you've taken, you're more of a coward than I was, because you're afraid to stand alone. If you haven't committed a crime, but enjoy disobeying and disrespecting your parents and teachers, drinking, using drugs, and having unprotected sex, you'll become addicted to whatever you use and end up with HIV. Your family, friends, and teachers will eventually get fed up as you walk down a negative and destructive path that leads to criminal behavior and eventually life imprisonment or death. Now ask yourself: Is it worth it?

The truth is anyone can end up in prison because of a bad choice. It happens every day to our favorite entertainers, sports figures, and even police officers – those who have taken an oath to protect and serve us. One of our presidents was even indicted. These examples should teach us that crime doesn't pay. If you do wrong, you are going down. You can't win, no matter how smart you think you are. Nothing is guaranteed in a life of crime but death or prison, so make the right choices. If you die after a life of crime, you will leave no legacy. No one will even remember your name.

If you end up in prison, you'll be put in a cold, lonely cell the size of a closet, told when to eat, when to sleep, when to go outside, what to wear, when to strip completely, and even what to say. You'll no longer be human; you'll be like an animal in a cage. At anytime, you could be cut, stabbed, or raped, while life and the world passes you by. You'll torture your family and community with your reckless actions. Once again, I ask you: Is it worth it? If you were fooled into a life of crime or if you are considering it, I beg you to think again. You're a unique and special person; you don't have to use drugs, sell drugs, or be in a gang to be accepted. I know it's hard out there and you're struggling, but there is no short cut to success.

Your dreams can come true. Believe in yourself and don't take life for granted. There are consequences for every bad decision. You can live a long, happy, productive, successful life or throw away your dreams for a one-way ticket to hell.

My name is Valentino Dixon, and I have spent the last fourteen years of my life in Attica Correctional Facility for a crime I didn't do. I spend my days in prison doing artwork. I was at the wrong place at the wrong time, but am I really innocent? And why should anyone care? I was a drug dealer, remember? Ask me: Was it worth it?

THIS IS A TRUESTORY!

Valentino Dixon,
Attica Correctional Facility

Which of these will be you?

Achievement = Success and happiness   **Jail = Pain and suffering**

CONTROLLING YOUR EMOTIONS

The dictionary defines **emotion** as an affective state of **consciousness** in which joy, sorrow, fear, hate, etc. is experienced. Emotion is an intense feeling. It can become so strong that it masters your judgment.

> **Young people, when you approach a problem, you allow your <u>emotions</u> to distort your judgment.**

1. Do you agree with this assumption? Yes__ No ___ Please explain:

_____
_____
_____
_____
_____

2. Do you believe that young people react to things emotionally first? Yes__ No __

3. Do you feel that the power of your emotions dominates reasoning? Yes __ No__

Please explain your answer:

_____
_____
_____
_____
_____

When you allow negative emotions to control you, you can become influenced by those who do not have your best interests at heart.

ACCORDING TO THE NATIONAL SEARCH INSTITUTE, ONE WAY TO BUILD SOCIAL COMPETENCIES IN YOUNG PEOPLE IS TO HELP THEM UNDERSTAND THE IMPORTANCE OF MAKING THE RIGHT CHOICES.

Building Social Competencies Using Forty Developmental Assets

Social competencies are the life skills that help young people grow to be healthy and…

- Be independent and capable of accomplishing your goals
- Learn how social competencies will equip you with the skills to relate to others
- Deal with the choices and challenges you face constructively
- Form and maintain healthy relationships with yourself and others
- Reduce or avoid stress and cope with it when it occurs in a positive manner
- Be effective in school and stay focused on the bigger picture

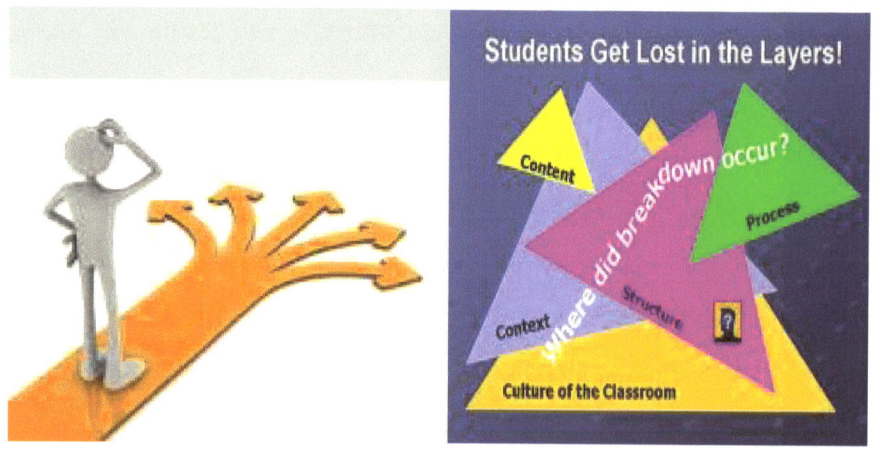

Developmental Assets® for Adolescents (ages 12-18)

The National Search Institute® has identified the following building blocks of healthy development, known as **Developmental Assets®**, which helps young people to grow up healthy, caring, and responsible.

External Assets 1-20

Support

1. Family Support—Family life provides high levels of love and support.
2. Positive Family Communication—The young person and her or his parent(s) communicate positively, and the young person is willing to seek advice and counsel from parents.
3. Other Adult Relationships—The young person receives support from three or more nonparent adults.
4. Caring Neighborhood—The young person experiences caring neighbors.
5. Caring School Climate—The school provides a caring, encouraging environment.
6. Parent Involvement in Schooling—Parent(s) are actively involved in helping the young person succeed in school.

Empowerment

7. The Community Values Youths—The young person perceives that adults in the community value youths.
8. Youth as Resources—Young people are given useful roles in the community.
9. Service to Others—The young person serves in the community one hour or more per week.
10. Safety—The young person feels safe at home, school, and in the neighborhood.

Boundaries and Expectations

11. Family Boundaries—The family has clear rules and consequences and monitors the young person's whereabouts.
12. School Boundaries—The school provides clear rules and consequences.
13. Neighborhood Boundaries—Neighbors take responsibility for monitoring young people's behaviors.
14. Adult Role Models—Parent(s) and other adults model positive, responsible behavior.
15. Positive Peer Influence—The young person's best friends model responsible behavior.
16. High Expectations—Both parent(s) and teachers encourage the young person to do well.

Constructive Use of Time

17. Creative Activities—The young person spends three or more hours per week in lessons or practice in music, theater, or other arts.
18. Youth Programs—The young person spends three or more hours per week in sports, clubs, or organizations at school and/or in the community.
19. Religious Community—The young person spends one or more hours per week in activities in a religious institution.
20. Time at Home—The young person is out with friends "with nothing special to do" two or fewer nights per week.

Internal Assets 21-40

Commitment to Learning

21. Achievement Motivation—The young person is motivated to do well in school.
22. School Engagement—The young person is actively engaged in learning.
23. Homework—The young person reports doing at least one hour of homework every school day.
24. Bonding to School—The young person cares about her or his school.
25. Reading for Pleasure—The young person reads for pleasure three or more hours per week.

Positive Values

26. Caring—The young person places high value on helping other people.
27. Equality and social justice—The young person places high value on promoting equality and reducing hunger and poverty.
28. Integrity—The young person acts on convictions and stands up for her or his beliefs.
29. Honesty—The young person "tells the truth, even when it is not easy."
30. Responsibility—The young person accepts personal responsibility.
31. Restraint—The young person believes it is important not to be sexually active or to use alcohol or other drugs.

Social Competencies

32. Planning and Decision Making—The young person knows how to plan ahead and make choices.
33. Interpersonal Competence—The young person has empathy, sensitivity, and friendship skills.
34. Cultural Competence—The young person has knowledge of and comfort with people of different cultural/racial/ethnic backgrounds.
35. Resistance Skills—The young person can resist negative peer pressure and dangerous situations.
36. Peaceful Conflict Resolution—The young person seeks to resolve conflict nonviolently.

Positive Identity

37. Personal Power—The young person feels he or she has control over things that happen.
38. Self-esteem—The young person reports having a high self-esteem.
39. Sense of Purpose—The young person reports that his or her life has a purpose.
40. Positive View of Future—The young person is optimistic about her or his future.

After reading over the assets above, create your own new assets, assets you can live with.

1. Take time to list some assets upon which you feel you can improve, assets that will make your life less complicated or confusing.

2. Then look at your situation and list how some assets will make you improve your circumstances.

Use this space below to start building your own assets:

How do you see your life moving forward? Who will you involve in your life?

How will you accomplish these assets?

Building my own assets	Who I will include in this process
_____	_____
_____	_____
_____	_____

_____/_____

_____/_____

_____/_____

_____/_____

_____/_____

_____/_____

_____/_____

Use the space below, if needed,

for additional asset building.

Self-Esteem

LESSON 3

By the end of this lesson, I will:

1) Examine the definition of self-esteem
2) Examine the characteristics of high self-esteem
3) Examine the characteristics of low self-esteem
4) Understand the importance of feeling good about myself

What is Self-Esteem?
1.

Self-esteem means loving and valuing yourself. It is a personal assessment of worthiness. Persons with high self-esteem appear poised and confident and are less influenced by their peers. This is different from being self-centered, conceited, or obnoxious. Building self-esteem is an ongoing process. It reaffirms that you have accepted yourself as you are, but will continue to work on capitalizing on your strengths.

2.
What is Low Self-esteem?

Everyone has low self-esteem at times. It may happen when someone says something bad about you or questions how well you do something, but if you often feel bad about yourself, you may stop believing in yourself. You may find it hard to move forward and accomplish anything.

3.
Characteristics of High Self-Esteem

An individual with high self-esteem feels good about him or herself and can face life's challenges more effectively. High self-esteem provides the basis for success and coping with a rapidly changing environment. You are the only person who can build your self-esteem; however, your family, parents, teachers, and friends can provide support and help influence many of your positive life choices.

I AM AWESOME

**Mr. Hotdog has very high self-esteem and confidence.
Take a long look at me, young people!
Ask yourself this question: Do I have what Mr. Hotdog has?**

- Self-esteem is the way we relate to ourselves, to others, and to life.
- It affects the way we learn, work, and build relationships.
- Our success or failure lies in our self-esteem.
- If you believe you can, you can; if you believe you can't, unfortunately, you don't even try. If you have high self-esteem, you are willing to try new things.
- You develop closer relationships and maintain self-confidence with high self-esteem.

High self-esteem will determine:

How you learn

How you work

How you act

How you think

How you react

How you interact

How you respond

All the above is determined by your level of self-esteem. Five factors are necessary to develop and maintain a high level of high self-esteem.

1. **Be a Positive Role Model** – Provide meaningful goals, values, ideals, and standards for yourself.
2. **Personal Strength** – Be a person with the ability to influence life's circumstances.
3. **Uniqueness and Individuality** – You have individual worth.
4. **Connectivity and Belonging** – You demonstrate a satisfaction from significant associations.
5. **Feeling Good about Yourself** – Thinking positively about who you are is the first step to having high self-esteem. Most people feel bad about themselves from time to time.

When answering the questions below, think about how you feel *most* of the time.

If you were able to relate to most of the questions above, you probably have a healthy opinion of yourself. However, if you were not able to relate to any of these questions, you have work to do.

> **The objective here is to work on your low self-esteem.
> Start building today. Use the tools you've
> been provide to start working today!**

Recap of Lesson 3

TEENS

Teens need to be able to maintain control of their lives and deal with peer pressure. Positive self-esteem can enable you to cope with the challenges and problems that are part of this pivotal stage. Self-reliant teens look to their futures with excitement and confidence while making plans to meet their life's goals.

MIDDLE/ JUNIOR HIGH SCHOOL/ ADOLESCENTS

Puberty presents quite a challenge for self-esteem! Yet, this time in your life can be exciting and wonderful. Certain building blocks are necessary for self-esteem to prosper. As adolescents, you need to feel approval, trust, acceptance, responsibility, self-respect, and a sense of power from others in order to grow into caring, competent, and contributing adults.

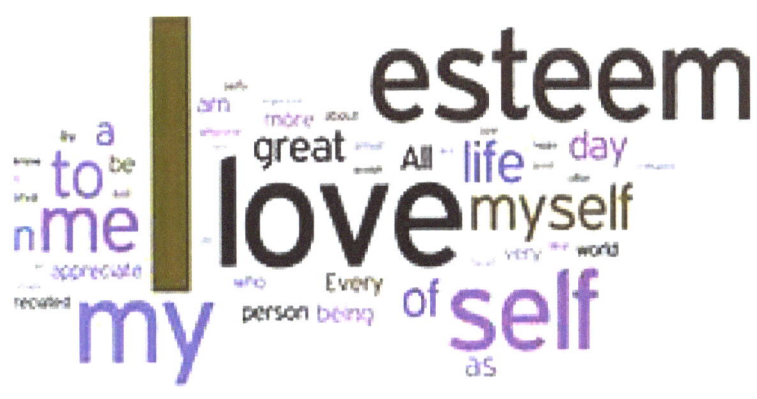

SUMMARY

Building better self-esteem is one of the most important things you can do for yourself. You can change your life by changing how you feel about yourself. Capitalizing on your strengths enables self-esteem to grow and prosper, regardless of your age. You should recognize and acknowledge your feelings, establish attainable goals, understand and respect yourself and others, identify your strengths, acknowledge your weaknesses, and appreciate your individual worth. Low self-esteem will keep you from accomplishing your goals. It can place you in a vulnerable situation where others will target you for bullying, fighting, or embarrassing you for no reason. If you suffer from low self-esteem, re-read this lesson until it starts to resonate. By following these suggestions, you will begin building self-esteem and start to become a person filled with joy and possibilities. Individuals with high self-esteem reach for the sky knowing that there is no limit on what they can accomplish.

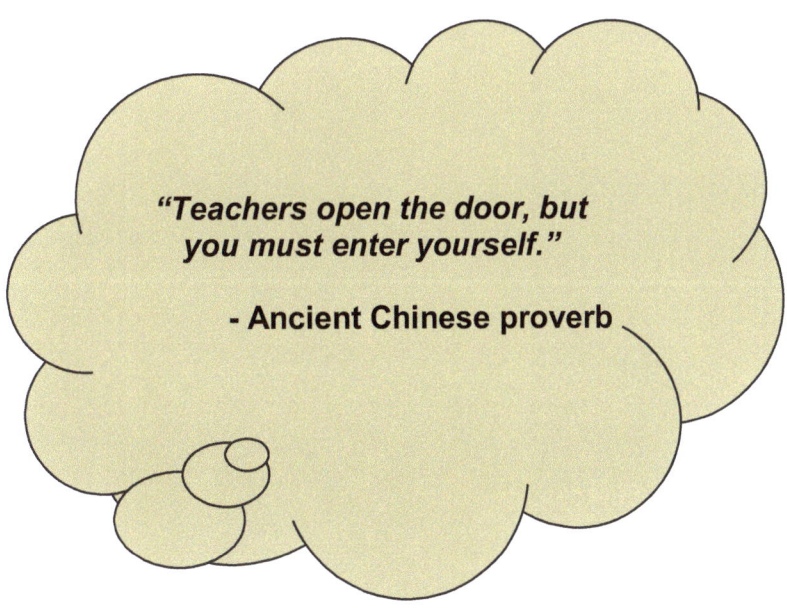

"Teachers open the door, but you must enter yourself."

- Ancient Chinese proverb

In-School Enrichment Curriculum
Self-Evaluation Activity
Read each question and answer each one with five words or less.

1. I like myself because:

   _____/_____/_____/_____/_____

2. I consider myself a good person because:

   _____/_____/_____/_____/_____

3. I am most happy when:

   _____/_____/_____/_____/_____

4. I like the way I feel about myself when:

   _____/_____/_____/_____/_____

5. My goals for the future are:

   _____/_____/_____/_____/_____

6. One of the most positive traits I have is:

   _____/_____/_____/_____/_____

7. My friends respect me because:

   _____/_____/_____/_____/_____

8. The person I look up to most is:

   _____/_____/_____/_____/_____

9. People say I am a good person because:

   _____/_____/_____/_____/_____

10. I have a natural talent for:

    _____/_____/_____/_____/_____

11. People say I have a good sense of human because:

    _____/_____/_____/_____/_____

12. The person that always makes me feel good about myself is:

    _____/_____/_____/_____/_____

13. I know that I will be successful in life because:

    _____/_____/_____/_____/_____

14. What I really enjoy most is:

    _____/_____/_____/_____/_____

15. People often compliment me about:

    _____/_____/_____/_____/_____

Comments/Reflection:
_____
_____
_____
_____
_____
_____
_____

Success Starts in Your Head

Whatever you focus on E X P A N D S,
and what you give energy to will become your reality.

Answer the following questions. If you have additional comments, please use the space below.

1. Are you honest and open about your feelings?   Yes___ No___

2. Are you happy for others when they are successful?   Yes___ No___

3. Do you accept constructive criticism and suggestions for improvement?   Yes___ No___

4. Are you at ease when you meet new people or are in new surroundings?   Yes___ No___

5. Are you able to laugh at yourself and learn from your mistakes?   Yes___ No___

6. Do you embrace change and look for new challenges?   Yes___ No___

7. Do you give yourself credit when credit is due?   Yes___ No___

8. Are you comfortable with your physical appearance?   Yes___ No___

9. Do you highly value your closest relationships with family and friends?   Yes___ No___

10. Do you enjoy quiet moments by yourself?   Yes___ No___

11. Do you value education?   Yes___ No___

12. Do you plan to graduate from high school?   Yes___ No___

13. Do you plan to go to college?   Yes___ No___

14. Will you be the first in your family to go to college?   Yes___ No___

15. Do you live with just one parent?   Yes___ No___

Use this space for additional comments:

Values

By the end of this lesson, I will:

1) Examine how values affect my behavior and my future.

2) Examine the benefits of upholding my family values that I have been taught.

3) Clearly identify my personal values.

LESSON 4

Introduction:

Do you understand the meaning of values?   Yes___ No ___

> **V**alues are a reflection of who you are, your culture, and your unique heritage. How will your values enable and empower you to establish priorities, make decisions you can live with, and build character that will serve you throughout your life?

Good **Values** will influence every stage of your life. Values shape what you believe in and perceive. Values influence your goals and help to select and rank your alternatives.

2. What Are Values?

Values are a part of your experience and affect your behavior. They determine your attitude, your standards for action, and your beliefs. Values are learned from family, your culture, and the people around you. In addition, values tell others what is important to you and what guides your decision making. You use your resources, like your time, money, and brainpower, on the things you value most.

3. Characteristics of Positive Values

Many of your ideals, beliefs, and behaviors are based on your values. Your values influence your thinking and behavior, your response to situations, how you carry yourself, how you respect yourself and others, how you learn, how you value education, and how you value your future. Can you think of anything else you should value? **Yes___ No ___**

Please explain your answer:

_____
_____
_____
_____
_____

LET'S DISCUSS SOME OTHER THINGS YOU VALUE

Exhibited Values...

- Become a guide for self-empowerment
- Help manage time, energy, and resources
- Help one to know oneself better
- Help eliminate confusion
- Help formulate a desired system of values
- Help one to behave in accordance with their values

Positive values...

- Promote honesty, integrity, commitment, and loyalty
- Encourage respect for self and others and tolerance of differences
- Require being responsible and accountable for your actions, while practicing self-control.
- Encourage fairness and treating people equally
- Foster consideration, kindness, compassion, and generosity toward others
- Foster good citizenship and appreciation for things that make life better

SUMMARY

Values are the "internal compasses" that guide you in developing priorities and making better choices. Although the internalization of values takes place over time, the groundwork is laid from the first day of life.

The foundation of character building begins during infancy and slowly evolves through childhood and adolescence, all the while becoming more sophisticated and complex. Individuals do not suddenly become honest and responsible when they become teenagers or adults. The development of these values is a long process that entails many interactions between children and adults.

Enrichment Self-Evaluation (What do you value?)

Values are important and personal. The point of this exercise is to determine what you actually value, not what you think you should value.

Below is a list of values. Look them over and circle all that are important to you. If something is important to you that you do not see on the list, write it in the space provided at the bottom.

Then rank your top five values in order of importance, 1 to 5. We will discuss your top five values and their meaning.

Look over this list carefully. Circle as many words or phrases as needed to reflect what it means to you.

Health	Commitment	Being Responsible	Wealth/Money
Helping	Others	Status	Beauty
Civic	Mindedness	Working	Integrity
Freedom	Being Special	Growth	Success
Recreation	Learning	Happiness	Wisdom
Intelligence	happiness	Family	Friendship
Being loved	Respect	Fairness	Family
Streets	Violence	Fighting	Gang Banging-
Bullying	Friends	Confidence	Determination
Honesty			

Now list values you did not see on this list under "Other Values, "then list the values you were able to identify as "Your Top Five Values."

OTHER VALUES:	MY TOP FIVE VALUES:
1._____	_____
2._____	_____
3._____	_____
4._____	_____
5._____	_____

Use the space below to further discuss what you value and why. Also, use this space to focus on new values you will try to develop.

Additional Comments/Reflection:

_____
_____
_____
_____
_____
_____
_____
_____
_____
_____
_____
_____
_____

> "If we don't change, we can't grow.
>
> If we don't grow, we aren't living
>
> --Gail Sheehy

HOW TO HANDLE CONFLICT

LESSON 5

By the end of this lesson, I will:

1) Understand the nature of conflicts
2) Identify my style of dealing with conflict
3) Learn ways to effectively resolve conflict with others.

1. The Nature of Conflict

Conflict—you'll find it everywhere, from the corporate world to the street corner. Whenever two people come into contact, the potential for conflict is there. It is a normal part of human interaction. Conflict arises when two people have different values or needs, and it appears that satisfying one person's needs might thwart the needs of the other. (Will you respect someone else's opinion even if you disagree on something, or will you stop talking to that person?) A solid friendship can have dilemmas, but **different values could be the source of the conflict.**

When you think about the word **"conflict,"** are your thoughts negative? A common belief is that conflict should be avoided. It is uncomfortable. **Have you ever considered that conflict can have benefits?**

2. Let's discuss the benefits of conflict:

Can we agree that conflict is not a sign of failure?   Yes __ No __
Can we agree that conflict can provide an opportunity for learning and improve relationships? Yes __ No __

Let's take the time to discuss points of view.

Look at this picture on the next page. What are your thoughts? Open discussion.

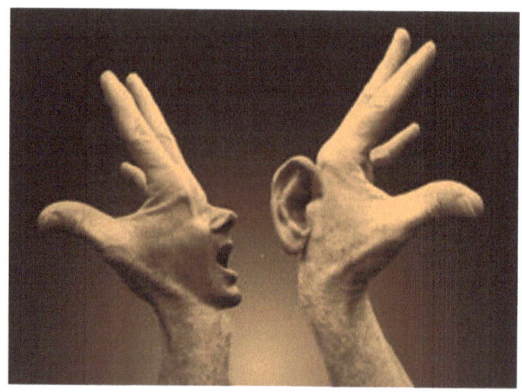

Are they having a disagreement, or are they just discussing something passionately? What do you think is taking place?

Let's look at how conflict can affect change:

Read each question and answer based on your beliefs about conflict and its impact.

* **Confrontation can lead to change?**

    Agree ___ Disagree ___ Not sure___

* **Being aware of conflicts can increase your motivation to do well.**

    Agree ___ Disagree___ Not sure___

* **Conflicts increase the awareness of problems.**

    Agree ___ Disagree___ Not sure___

* **Conflicts make life more interesting.**

    Agree ___ Disagree___ Not sure___

* **Disagreement often causes a decision to be thought through more carefully.**

    Agree ___ Disagree___ Not sure___

* **Conflicts help you understand what you are like under pressure.**

    Agree ___ Disagree___ No___

* **Minor conflict can defuse potentially large ones?**

    Agree ___ Disagree___ No___

CONFLICTS CAN BE FUN IF THEY ARE NOT TAKEN TOO SERIOUSLY.

Conflict can provide you with some directions and opportunities for growth. **Can you capitalize on the positives and make conflict work for you?   Yes __ No__**

Please explain your answer.

_____
_____
_____
_____
_____
_____
_____
_____
_____
_____
_____
_____
_____
_____

How would you say you deal with conflict? (What's your style?)

Read each question carefully, place a check mark beside characteristics you feel best describe how you deal with conflict. Do this activity individually. Be honest with yourself. It does not matter how many you check off. Remember, there is no right or wrong answer.

"Do You" List

Do you:

- Try to overpower opponents by forcing them to accept your solution to a conflict?   ___
- Consider your goals of high importance and the relationship of minor importance?   ___
- Seek to achieve your goals at all costs?   ___
- Assume conflicts are settled by one person winning and one person losing?   ___
- Attempt to win by overpowering or intimidating others?   ___
- Seek a compromise?   ___
- Give up part of your goals and persuade other people to give up part of his/her goals?   ___
- Sacrifice part of your goal to find agreement for the common good?   ___
- Feel the relationship is of great importance, while your own goals are of little importance?   ___
- Want to be accepted and liked by others?   ___
- Think that conflict should be avoided in favor of harmony?   ___
- Believe that conflicts cannot be discussed without damaging relationships?   ___
- Give up your goals to preserve a relationship?   ___
- Withdraw into a shell to avoid conflicts?   ___
- Give up personal goals and relationships to avoid conflicts?   ___
- Avoid conflicts and people you are in conflict with.   ___
- Feel it is hopeless to try to resolve conflicts?   ___
- Believe it easier to withdraw (physically and psychologically) from a conflict than to face it?   ___
- Highly value your own goals and relationships?   ___
- Seek a solution that achieves both your goals and the goals of the other person?   ___
- See conflict as improving relationships by reducing tension between you and others?   ___

Count the number of check marks. Put the total here _____

Before you read the personalities below, try to keep these three outcomes for conflict in mind while reading each one!

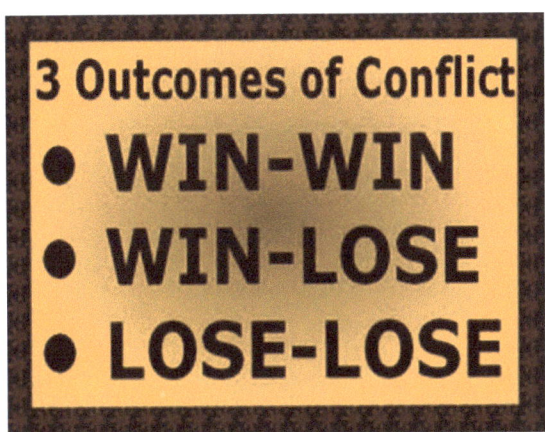

Read the different personality styles and determine which of the characters best represents your personality.

Take your time and read over each one carefully. You may find that you are more than one of personality style.

   Picture yourself as a shark_____.

A. Sharks tend to use force, causing the other side to give in. This creates a winner and a loser. The shark has a deep personal interest in the outcome of the conflict, but does not care much about the needs of others involved.

   Picture yourself as fox_____.

B. Foxes use compromise, or bargaining behavior, in which each side obtains part of what it wants. An attempt is made to find an answer in which the gains and losses of both parties are equal. This style leaves the interests and needs of each person only partially satisfied.

Picture yourself as a teddy bear_____.

C. Teddy bears tend to smooth things over and fail to confront areas of conflict. This person probably does not have as much personal interest or stake in the conflict, but does care about the needs of others.

Picture yourself as a turtle_____.

D. Turtles withdraw to avoid conflict situations entirely. Little attempt is made to satisfy either their personal needs or the needs of others.

Picture yourself as an owl_____.

E. Owls use problem-solving behavior in which both sides have their needs met at a level sufficient to avoid feelings of losing. Everyone wins; conflict is reduced or eliminated. This style requires understanding all viewpoints.

It's not uncommon for you to have a few characteristics or several styles or more than one style. You may see yourself behaving differently depending on the person with whom you are in conflict.

This exercise can provide you an opportunity to look at your different behavior in different situations.

Now that you have learned more about your style(s) and characteristic(s) when dealing with conflict, do you think that choosing collaboration for solving your problems is a possibility going forward? Yes_____ No _____ Not sure _____

Please explain your answer.

_____
_____
_____
_____

Collaboration promotes an understanding of:

- Perspective
- Increased communication
- Cooperation
- Interdependence
- Integrity
- Trust
- Mutual support

> Now that you know a little more about the characteristics of handling conflict, let's discuss skills you can use to manage conflict.

Author **James Rick** said, "**A problem not well-defined is half solved.**"

4. Managing Conflict

Below, we discuss some ways you can consider resolving conflict.

1. State the problem. Ask yourself, "What is the problem?"
2. Be as specific as possible, giving attention to as many aspects of the problem as possible.
3. Have you thought about separating the problem from how you are really feeling?
   Yes ___ No ___ Haven't given it any thought ___
4. Could something else **be the real problem**?
   Yes ___ No ___ Haven't given it any thought ___

Let's discuss your answer to this question in more detail.

Other questions to ask yourself as you define problems with conflict:

- How do I know it is a problem?
- Is the situation the problem or is my reaction to the situation a problem?
- Is there more than one problem?
- Why is it a problem?
- If nothing is done, what will happen? (Is there really a problem?)

Use the exercise below to help you solve problems better. You will learn how using better life or social skills can avoid negative conflict.

Conflict can be helpful if... **(Answer after you have had a chance to read below.)**

- You are able to work better with others after the conflict because you have respect for their opinion.
- You and the others involved feel better about each other after the conflict because you take down the wall.
- You and the others are satisfied with the results of the conflict because you found ways to learn from it.
- Your ability to resolve future conflicts with others has been enhanced because you see things differently.
- You know more about the issue and understand how the discussion can be resolved in a positive way.
- You feel your point of view has been heard and you can respect the other person's point of view.

Questions:

1. **Some people feel that compromise is an effective method for dealing with conflict.** True_____ False_____

    Please explain your answer to this question before moving to the next questions.

    _____
    _____
    _____
    _____

2. **Why is collaboration a more effective method?**

    _____
    _____
    _____
    _____

3. **A friend recently mentioned to you that he/she tries to avoid conflict at all costs. What would you say to him/her about conflict?**

    _____
    _____
    _____
    _____

4. What do you think is the root of all conflict?

_____
_____
_____
_____

Answers:

1. Although compromise can be useful, it can also build frustration and mistrust. The parties involved may become frustrated when their needs are only partially met. **Collaboration, openness, and honesty are always encouraged.** This approach seeks to meet everyone's needs; information is shared freely and without suspicion. Power is shared equally.
2. Although we think of conflict as negative, there can be some positive aspects. For example, conflict can lead to change and motivate you to do your best. It can also cause a decision to be thought out more carefully. Life could be pretty boring without some conflict.
3. Conflict between people develops when there is a struggle over values and claims to scarce status, power, or resources. When two people have different values or goals and it is perceived that satisfying one person's needs will directly thwart the other person from meeting his or her needs, conflict develops.

Additional Comments and/Reflections:

_____
_____
_____
_____
_____
_____
_____
_____
_____
_____
_____
_____
_____
_____
_____

This is where you want to be after any disagreement with others!

Never end a conflict mad, upset, or still confused.

It's not fair for either person.

Always walk away with a clear understanding and a

WIN/WIN OUTCOME.

Peer Pressure

LESSON 6

By the end of this lesson, I will be able to:

1. Clearly define peer pressure
2. Discuss positive and negative forms of peer pressure
3. Explain ways to resist negative peer pressure
4. Understand the importance of speaking out against negative peer pressure

1. PeerPressure

"Come on! All of us are cutting math today! Who wants to take that quiz anyway? We're going to take a walk and get lunch, instead. Let's go!" says the smoothest kid in your class.

- Will you do what you know is wrong?   Yes___ No ___
- Are you thinking that maybe you will take the bait this time?   Yes___ No ___
- Will you do what is right and take your math quiz?   Yes___ No ___
- Are you really thinking about doing what is right?   Yes___ No ___

As we explore peer pressure further, please be prepared to respond.

Making decisions on your own is hard, but when other people try to pressure you one way or another, deciding on a course of action gets much more difficult. Students in your age group, like classmates, friends, cousins, etc., will try to influence how you act, get you to do things you may not be comfortable with, or get you to do things about which you really don't feel good. This behavior is called "**peer pressure**." It's something everyone deals with, especially in school settings. Even adults deal with peer pressure. Let's identify different forms of peer pressure.

2. Different Forms of Pressure:

<u>Negative Peer Pressure</u> – Negative peer pressure comes in many forms. One form is rejection. Have you ever been rejected? Yes __ No ___ If <u>yes,</u> please explain how it made you feel. Please explain your answer:

_____
_____
_____
_____

Rejection:

Do you think rejection can threaten or end a friendship or relationship? Yes __ No __
Check your answer and be prepared to explain below:

_____
_____
_____
_____

Some examples of peer pressure by rejection...

We will discuss and do some role-playing for this session of the training.

- ➢ Who needs you as a friend, anyway?
- ➢ If you don't drink, you don't need to hang out with us anymore.
- ➢ Why don't you leave if you don't want to join us?
- ➢ Have you ever suffered from "put downs," especially in front of a group?
- ➢ Have you been insulted or been called names to make you feel bad?

Have you ever experienced any of the following?

- You're never fun   Yes____   No ____
- You're such a baby   Yes____   No ____
- You're such a punk.   Yes____   No ____
- You just don't know how to be cool at all.   Yes____   No ____
- You look funny   Yes____   No ____
- Why do you always smell so bad   Yes____   No ____
- Why do you dress like that   Yes____   No ____

Negative Peer Pressure:

> Here are examples of how peers influence each other in negative ways. Kids in school might try to get you to cut class with them, friends in your neighborhood might want you to join a local gang, or shoplift with them. You may even be pressured into having sex. These are all forms of negative peer pressure, but peer pressure is not always negative. Let's now examine forms of positive peer pressure.

Positive Peer Pressure:

> Peers can have a positive influence on each other. Maybe a student in your science class taught you an easy way to remember the planets in the solar system, or someone on the basketball team taught you a new move on the court. You might admire a friend who is always a good sport and try to be more like him or her. Maybe you got others excited about your new favorite book, and now everyone's reading it. These are examples of how peers positively influence each other every day.

You and your friends can also pressure each other into things that will improve your health and social life and make you feel good about your decisions. Think of a time when a friend pushed you to do something good for yourself or avoid something bad. **Here are some good things friends can pressure each other to do:**

* Be honest	* Avoid alcohol	* Avoid drugs
* Don't smoke	* Be nice	* Respect others
* Work hard	*Study hard	*Say thank you

You and your friends can also use good peer pressure to help each other resist bad peer pressure. If you see a friend experiencing negative pressure, try some of these lines:

- We don't want to drink.
- We don't need to drink to have fun.
- Let's do something else.
- Leave her alone. She said she didn't want any.
- I am going to do my school work. Why don't you, as well?
- Maybe you need to hang out with new friends.
- You really should think before allowing them to make you do something you don't really want to do.

- Don't allow someone to talk you into skipping class. Don't you want to graduate?
- You should turn in your homework and not worry about others talking about how smart you are.

We have examined different forms of "spoken peer pressure." Now we are going to review unspoken peer pressure.

> There are times you might think you are supposed to act or dress a certain way because everyone else is doing it, or because it's the cool thing to do. When you feel this way, even though nobody has said anything to you about it, this is

> If you haven't already, it's very possible that you will face both spoken and unspoken pressure in the future. It's just a part of life. The most important thing is to make the right choices when under

1. How to Handle Peer Pressure

- Some kids give in to peer pressure because they want to be liked.

    Agree _____ Disagree _____

- To fit in, you may have to compromise your own beliefs.

    Agree _____ Disagree _____

- Students may make fun of you if they don't go along with what they want you to do.

    Agree _____ Disagree _____

- Others may go along because they are curious to try something new.

    Agree _____ Disagree _____

- The idea that everyone is doing it influence kids to go against their better judgment.

    Agree _____ Disagree _____

- It is tough to be the only one who say "no" to peer pressure.

    Agree _____ Disagree _____

- Trusting your own beliefs about what is right and wrong is the right thing to do.

    Agree _____ Disagree _____

> **Inner strength and self-confidence can help you stand firm, walk away, and resist doing something when you know better.**

2. Resisting Peer-Pressure

Do you think that having at least one other peer or friend who is willing to say no will make it easier for you to say no, also? Yes___ No ___

Please explain your answer and be prepared to discuss it:

_____
_____
_____
_____
_____

Do you think it's great to have friends with values similar to yours, who will back you up when you don't want to do something? Yes_____ No _____

Please explain your answer. Be prepared to discuss it with the group.

_____
_____
_____
_____
_____

> **You've probably had a parent or teacher advise, "Choose your friends wisely." Peer pressure is why they say this. If you choose friends who don't use drugs, cut class, smoke cigarettes, or lie to their parents, then you probably won't do these things, either, even if other kids do. Try to help a friend who's having trouble resisting peer pressure. It can be powerful for one kid to simply say, "I'm with you. Let's go."**

Even if you're faced with peer pressure while you're alone, there are things you can do. You can simply say no and know it's okay to say no to peers who want you to do things you know are wrong. You can tell them no and walk away.

Better yet, find other friends and classmates.

If you continue to face peer pressure and find it difficult to handle, talk to someone you trust. Don't feel guilty if you've made a mistake or two. Talking to a parent, a teacher, a friend or a school counselor can help you feel better and prepare you for the next time you're faced with peer pressure.

Summary

Peer pressure influences your life, even if you don't realize it, just by spending time with others. You learn from them, and they learn from you. It's human nature to listen to and learn from other people in your age group.

If someone is pressuring you to do things that are not right or good for you, you have the **right to resist.** You have **the right to say no, the right not to give a reason why,** and the **right to walk away from a situation**. Sometimes resisting isn't easy, but you can do it with practice and a little know-how. Keep trying, even if you don't get it right at first. To get started, check out these Quick Tips.

Quick Tips: You can resist alcohol, drugs, or anything else you may feel pressured into doing. These tips will make resisting a little easier. Print it, cut it out, stash it somewhere safe where you can peek at it if you need it, **THEN USE IT.**

Quick Tips on Resisting Peer Pressure:

1. Say no, and mean it.

2. Stand up straight.

3. Say how you feel.

4. Don't make excuses.

5. Stick up for yourself.

Additional Comments/Reflection:

_____
_____
_____
_____
_____

Pressure – the feeling that you are being pushed toward making a certain choice – either good or bad.

Peer – someone in your own age group.

Peer Pressure – the feeling that someone your own age is pushing you toward a certain choice, good or bad.

REMEMBER:

YOU CONTROL PEER PRESSURE;

PEER PRESSURE DOES NOT CONTROL YOU

UNLESS

YOU ALLOW IT.

Gang Affiliation

LESSON 7

By the end of this lesson, I will:

1) Clearly define what a gang is
2) Examine the reasons why people join gangs
3) Examine the personal effects of being in a gang
4) Examine how being in a gang affects my family
5) Examine how gangs affect my community
6) Discuss my feelings about being in a gang

1. What is a Gang?

Most commonly, the word "gang" refers to street groups (a.k.a. youth gangs), groups of school-age kids who form an allegiance for a common purpose and often engage in violent criminal activities. They are also known for claiming certain territories to be "their turf" in different communities.

Some more structured gangs have members who assume leadership roles. Leadership roles in street gangs are usually not formally recognized positions. They are, however, the dominant control factor in the gang, and they often require members to perform certain activities to impress other members. Gangs are usually comprised of males ranging from nine to twenty-eight years of age. Girls are not excluded from gang activities, and studies show that girl gangs have become more of a problem than in past generations.

2. Levels of Gang Involvement

REGULARS: Gang members who "hang out" with the group on a regular basis

HARD CORE: More deeply committed gang members' usually responsible for instigating and committing the most serious offenses attributed to their gang

ASSOCIATES: Friends, acquaintances, and relatives who are somewhat knowledgeable about gang activities and who occasionally

3. Why Join a Gang?

Young people from various ethnic and socio-economic groups join gangs. No ethnic group or geographical location is excluded. Interviews with gang members indicate that the reasons for joining are seldom understood by the gang members themselves, but can vary from brotherhood and sisterhood inside the gang to self-preservation. Listed below are some of the main reasons young people join gangs:

1. **Identity**: Gang members may not be able to identify with their own environment, so they turn to the gang culture. They often visualize themselves as warriors against the outside world, protecting their neighborhoods.
2. **Protection:** In a community with several existing gangs, joining one seems to offer protection from violence and attacks from rival gangs.
3. **Fellowship**: Studies indicate that most gang members do not have tight family structures. Gang activity offers closeness and a sense of family sometimes lacking in the home.
4. **Intimidation**: Threats, violent beatings, and dangerous initiations are often used to force people to join.
5. **Self-Esteem**: Sometimes students with poor self-esteem want recognition for their activities. Criminal or not, gangs supply an extra pat on the back that may not be given at home or in school. Many do not realize the hazards involved in gang activity.
6. **Other Reasons:** There are varieties of reasons why young people join gangs. They include the excitement of gang activity, a need to belong, peer pressure, attention, financial gain, and sometimes gang family tradition. The lack of strong **parental** involvement in a child's life can leave the child feelings secluded, alone, and unwanted, which makes the child a ***prime target for gang affiliation.***
7. **Lack of Positive Parental Involvement:** If the parents never learned adequate parenting skills, it is unlikely they will be able to achieve positive parental involvement in the child's life. This means the child may struggle with **low self-esteem, poor communication skills, and poor decision making skills**. All these factors contribute to a desperate craving within the child for acceptance, recognition, and respect. In other words, the gang gives them what they lack at home.
8. **Negative Relationship to the Community**: Although low self-esteem, poor communication skills, and poor decision making skills originate in the family, their effects carry over into the child's relationship to the community and affects his or her ability to resist negative influences outside the home. Within the community, they may result in low grades, poor school attendance, little or no involvement in extracurricular school activities, and little or no involvement in community based programs.

The Gang Member's Family:
In addition to the stress of worrying about the gang member in the family, the family has the added stress of knowing their welfare and safety are threatened. When one child in a family is a member of a gang, the risk of brothers and sisters joining a gang will be greatly

increased. Even when the gang member's parents, sisters, and brothers have nothing to do with gangs, rival gangs frequently target the family and their property (i.e. assaults and vandalism). Very often, innocent people are disliked, beaten, or even gunned down simply because they were the family of a gang participant.

Making the Transition

Former hard-core gang members decided to change their lives around. The greatest challenges they had to face and some of the things they regretted the most were:

- **I regret dropping out of school, and now that I have a child and see life differently, it is hard to find a job even worth working.**
- **I regret the pain that I caused my family and other families in my community, and the memories of the things I have done will be with me for the rest of my life.**
- **Now that I have changed my life around, I don't hustle or gangbang anymore. I need to get a job, but I am afraid to work because I fear someone that I have wronged will do something to me**
- **One of the greatest challenges I am faced with is trying to make up for all of the time I lost while in jail. After the last six years I spent in jail, I feel like a fool. I at least could have earned my G.E.D. or a college degree while I was in there, but all I did was gangbang while I was there, and all I left with was forty-two stitches in my face. Now I have two felonies on my record, no education, a scar across my face for the rest of my life, and if I don't get a job soon, I'll have nowhere to stay, but I am determined not to give up and return to my old lifestyle.**

"40 Developmental Assets Offered by the National Search Institute" provides ways you can keep young people from ever desiring to join a gang. Some of the developmental assets greatly needed to deter gang affiliation are:

1. <u>**Strong support system**</u>: family who provides a high level of love and support
2. <u>**Good communication**</u>: Good communication is open and frequent. It has a positive tone. It allows children to open up with concerns and issues. It does not condemn or put down. It includes telling and showing support.
3. **Time with positive role models**: Plan activities the whole family can enjoy. Also, spend time alone with each child individually. Spend time with friends doing things that are safe and fun. Get involved with different organizations that provide afterschool programs.
4. **Occupy your child/referee time**. Parents should give their child more responsibilities at home.

Be honest when answering each question. This information will not be used against you in anyway. After you complete all questions, we will discuss each in a group discussion. Remember, there is no right or wrong answers.

☐ What are your likes and dislikes about gang activities?
_____
_____
_____
_____

☐ Activities do you participate in outside the home?
_____
_____
_____
_____

☐ How do you spend your spare time at home?
_____
_____
_____
_____

☐ Are you skipping school to attend gang activities?
_____
_____
_____
_____

☐ Are you using alcohol or drugs?
_____
_____
_____
_____

☐ **Do you go home bruised or injured?**

_____
_____
_____
_____

When you go out at night, do your parents or your guardian know where you are? Or do they know who you are with, and their name? Yes____ No ____

Please explain your answer and be prepared to discuss:

_____
_____
_____
_____
_____
_____
_____
_____
_____
_____
_____
_____
_____
_____
_____
_____

Joining a gang is not hip. It's not safe. It's not cool. It's not healthy. It doesn't represent you! You deserve better. You have too many good things waiting for you. Here is a good gang to join. It's called, "Me, myself, and I." If you really just have to join a gang, change what a gang can stands for. Peace and Love

Group Discussions:

- **Have you ever been associated or affiliated with a gang?**

    Yes_____ No_____ will not disclose _____

    If yes, what were your reasons for joining?

    _____
    _____
    _____
    _____
    _____

- **If you have never been involve with a gang, why not?**

    _____
    _____
    _____
    _____
    _____

❖ What are some of your reasons for wanting to be a part of a gang?

_____
_____
_____
_____
_____

❖ What are some perceived benefits for being a member of a gang? What are some of the disadvantages?

_____
_____
_____
_____
_____

❖ How do you think gang activities affect the community in which you live? How do you think gang members are perceived by adults in the community?

_____
_____
_____
_____
_____

❖ After becoming a member of a gang, how easy do you think it is to disassociate yourself from the gang?

_____
_____
_____
_____
_____

❖ Is it true that once you join a gang you are likely to start using drugs and alcohol?

❖ Do you believe that all gangs engage in violent and destructive activities?

❖ How do you think gang activities affect an individual's family?

❖ Do you think being in a gang has a negative or positive effect on school?

❖ **If you do belong to a gang, is there anything in your life for which you would be willing to quit the gang?**

_____
_____
_____
_____
_____

Additional comments/Reflection:

_____
_____
_____
_____
_____
_____
_____
_____
_____
_____
_____
_____
_____
_____
_____
_____
_____
_____

BULLYING HURTS

By the end of this lesson, I will:

1) Understand the importance of increasing my self-esteem

2) How to stand up to bullies

3) How to identify the signs of becoming bullied

4) How to identify students who bully others

Stop! Bullying HURTS:

Bullying is a widespread and serious problem that can happen anywhere. It is not a phase children go through, it is not "just messing around," and it is not something to grow out of. Bullying can cause serious and lasting harm to others.

> Although definitions of bullying vary, most agree that bullying is increasingly recognized as one of the worst problems affecting the well-being and social functioning of students. While a certain amount of conflict and harassment is typical in peer relations, bullying represents a potentially more serious threat

A List of Negative and Aggressive Bully Behaviors:

1) The behavior is intended to harm or disturb another person for no reason.
2) The behavior occurs repeatedly over time.
3) There is an imbalance of power, with a more powerful person or group attacking a less powerful person.
4) There is intent to cause harm.
5) Physical: hitting, punching, and shoving

Use the space below to discuss the bullying specifics

How do you think you would feel if you were ever a victim of a bully?

Explain what you would do if you witnessed someone being victimized?

Have you ever been bullied? Yes__ No__

Please explain how all this makes you feel:
_____
_____
_____
_____

> A study conducted by: Leonard Eron and Rowell Huesman states:" Young bullies carry a one-in-four chance of having a criminal record by the age 30."
> A Study conducted by Dan Olweus, National School Safety Center, states: "American schools harbor approximately 2.1 million bullies and 2.7 million of their victims."

Avoid Becoming a Bully:

Students must be proactive in identifying supportive and caring peer relationships. Friendship is a shared and equal relationship. **Unfortunately**, in an unequal relationship, you will probably feel pressured to be accepted because you really want so badly to be able to fit into a group.

Let's examine some characteristic Bully Behaviors.

Students who bully other students are likely to demonstrate several of the following:

- A positive attitude toward violence and the use of violent means

- A strong need to dominate and subdue other students to get their own way

- A tendency to be impulsive and easily angered

- Little empathy toward students who are bullied

- Defiance and aggression towards adults, including teachers and parents

- Involvement in antisocial or rule-breaking activities, such as vandalism, delinquency, and substance abuse

How to Handle Teasing by a Bully

Behavior of a Bully:

- Teasing someone on the bus because the person is "nerdy"
- Taking someone's dessert in the cafeteria
- Excluding someone from a game at recess
- Gossiping about someone's clothes

Suggested Reaction:

- Don't react. Walk away, don't cry, and ignore the bully.
- Smile or laugh. If you do the opposite of what the bully expects, the bully doesn't have any fun.
- Communicate. Tell the teaser calmly how you feel. When you're calm, bullying loses its power.
- Inform an adult. If you need help, ask for it. **That's not tattling; that's standing up for yourself.**

> At this point, we will stop and do some role-playing.

EFFECTS OF CYBER-BULLYING

Cyber-bullying doesn't happen face-to-face; it happens using technology, such as computers, cell phones, and other electronic devices. Cyber-bullying peaks around the end of middle school and the beginning of high school.

Examples of cyber-bullying include:

- Sending hurtful, rude, or mean text messages to others
- Spreading rumors or lies about others via e-mail or social networks
- Creating websites, videos or social media profiles that embarrass, humiliate, or make fun of others

Bullying online is very different from face-to-face bullying because messages and images can be:

- ✓ Sent 24 hours a day, 7 days a week, 365 days a year
- ✓ Shared to a very wide audience
- ✓ Sent anonymously

Research on cyber-bullying has found that students being cyber-bullied are more likely to:

- ✓ Be unwilling to attend school
- ✓ Receive poor grades
- ✓ Have lower self-esteem
- ✓ Have more health problems

Suggestions for Texting and Being Online

You can prevent cyber-bullying by being careful what you say and do:

1. **Always think about what you post or say.** Do not share secrets, photos, or anything that might be embarrassing to you or others. What seems funny or innocent could be used against you. You do not have control over what others forward or post.

2. **Set privacy settings on your accounts.** Make sure that you are only sharing information with people you know and trust. Pay attention to notices from social networks, because sometimes privacy settings change.

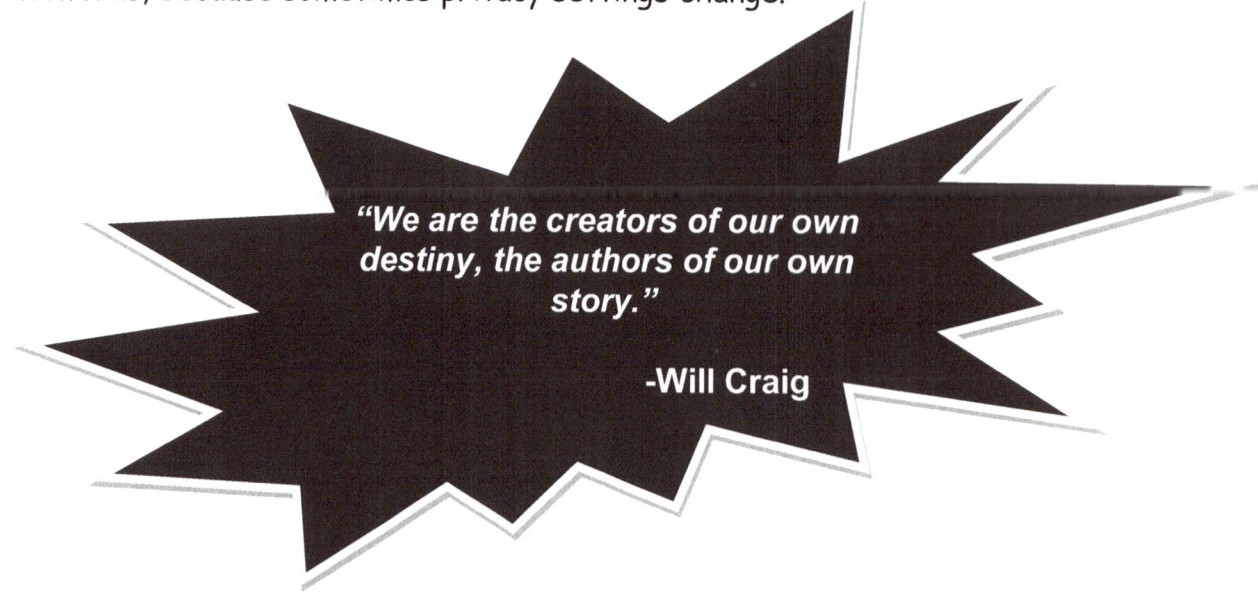

"We are the creators of our own destiny, the authors of our own story."

-Will Craig

Anti-Bullying Reflection Questions for Group Discussion:

1. **Do you think bullying is a serious problem in your school or community?**

    Yes____ No_____ I don't know _____

    Please explain your answer.

    _____
    _____
    _____
    _____
    _____

2. **How do you think bullies feel when they demean someone else?**

    Good____ Bad____ Not Sure _____

    Please explain your answer and be prepared to discuss it.

    _____
    _____
    _____
    _____
    _____

3. **Do you think it's possible to make a bully understand other people's feelings?**

    Yes____ No_____ I don't know _____

    Please explain your answer.

    _____
    _____
    _____
    _____
    _____

4. **How do parents and adults in your school or community address bullying?**

    _____
    _____
    _____
    _____
    _____

What kind of interventions have you seen adults use to prevent or stop bullying? Please explain your answer.

_____
_____
_____
_____
_____

5. **What kind of interventions can you use to prevent or stop bullying? List three things you would do to defuse a situation.**

   _____/_____/_____

6. **Did any of the facts in this lesson concern you personally?**

   Yes____ No____

   Please explain why:

   _____
   _____
   _____
   _____
   _____

7. **Are there behaviors or experiences you have had that you want to change?**

   Yes ____ No____

   Describe your feelings, what you would like to change, and then describe the actions you would take to make these changes. **Dig Deep:**

   _____
   _____
   _____
   _____
   _____

Recognizing Warning Signs:

There are many warning signs that could indicate that someone is bullying others or being bullied. However, below are some warning signs you should be aware of. Share this information with your teachers, parents, and friends.

ADDITIONAL SIGNS OF BEING BULLIED:

- Comes home with damaged or missing clothing or other belongings
- Reports losing items such as books, electronics, clothing, or jewelry
- Has unexplained injuries
- Complains frequently of headaches, stomachaches, or feeling sick
- Has trouble sleeping or frequent bad dreams
- Has changes in eating habits
- Hurts him or herself
- Are very hungry after school (from not eating his or her lunch)
- Runs away from home
- Loses interest in visiting or talking with friends
- Is afraid of going to school or other activities with peers
- Loses interest in schoolwork or begins to do poorly in school
- Appears sad, moody, angry, anxious, or depressed when he or she come home
- Talks about suicide
- Feels helpless
- Often feels like he or she is not good enough
- Blames self for his or her problems
- Suddenly have fewer friends
- Avoids certain places
- Acts different

Please use this section to record how *Life Skills* has changed you and how you will use your skills to help others build life skills.

List of References and Footnotes:

Swihart, 198,
John Wooden,
Augustus Napier
French Proverb
Jacqueline Mines, Helping Families and children
Aldous Huxley,
Ralph Waldo Emerson
Virginia Satir
Henry Ford,
Moliére, pg.
Martin Luther King, Jr.
Leonard Eron and Rowell Huesman,
Lee Iacocca,
Justice Louis D. Brandeis,
James Rick,
Valentino Dixon, Attica Correctional Facility
AlfieKoj,n
Priscilla Prutzman,
Dr. Peter Scales of Search Institute,
Dr. Peter Benson of Search Institute,
National Search Institute,
Karen J. Pittman,
40 Developmental Assets by the National Search Institute,
Dan Olweus, National School Safety Center,
Research Engines of various sites, and books
Mother Teresa, Insert
Scoot Master and Andy Gibbs, Insert

1. Levy, F., &Murname, R. (1992). US earnings levels and earning inequality: A review of recent trends and proposed explanations. Journal of Economic Literature, 30, 1332-1381.
2. Spoth, R.L., Randall, G., Trudeau, L., Shin, C., & Redmond, C. (2008). Substance use outcomes 5½ years past baseline for partnership-based, family school prevention interventions. Drug and Alcohol Dependence, 96, 57-68.
3. Botvin, G.J., Griffin, K.W., Diaz, T., &Ifill-Williams, M. (2001). Drug abuse prevention among minority adolescents: Posttest and one-year follow-up of a school-based prevention intervention. Prevention Science, 2(1), 1-13.
4. Botvin, G.J., Baker, E., Dusenbury, L., Tortu, S., &Botvin E.M. (1990). Preventing adolescent drug abuse through a multimodal cognitive-behavioral approach: Results of a three-year study. Journal of Consulting and Clinical Psychology, 58, 437-446.
5. Griffin, K.W., Botvin, G.J., & Nichols, T.R. (2006). Effects of a school-based drug abuse prevention program for adolescents on HIV risk behaviors in young adulthood. Prevention Science, 7, 103-112.
6. Botvin, G.J., Griffin, K.W., & Nichols, T.R. (2006). Preventing youth violence and delinquency through a universal school-based prevention approach. Prevention Science, 7, 403-408.
7. Botvin et al. (2001).
8. Engberg, J., &Morral, A.R. (2006). Reducing substance use improves adolescents' school attendance. Addiction, 101, 1741-1751.
9. National Center for Chronic Disease Prevention and Health Promotion (2009, July 29). Fact Sheet: Student Health and Academic Achievement. Retrieved 25 August, 2009 from the Center for Disease Control website: http://www.cdc.gov/HealthyYouth/health_and_academics/#5.
10. Grossman, J.B. & Cooney, S.M. (2009). Paving the way for success in high school and beyond: The Importance.

www.ingramcontent.com/pod-product-compliance
Lightning Source LLC
Chambersburg PA
CBHW042032150426
43200CB00002B/27